W9-BYE-948

If I Only Had a Horn
Young Louis Armstrong

Roxane Orgill

Illustrated by Leonard Jenkins

Houghton Mifflin Company
Boston

For Valerie Worth
—R.O.

This picture book is for my mother, Beverly Jenkins
—L.J.

Text copyright © 1997 by Roxane Orgill
Illustrations copyright © 1997 by Leonard Jenkins

All rights reserved. For information about permission to reproduce
selections from this book, write to Permissions, Houghton Mifflin Company,
215 Park Avenue South, New York, New York 10003.

For information about this and other Houghton Mifflin trade and reference
books and multimedia products, visit The Bookstore
at Houghton Mifflin on the World Wide Web at http://www.hmco.com/trade/.

The text of this book is set in 16 point Janson Text.
The illustrations are acrylic, pastel, and spray paint, reproduced in full color.

Library of Congress Cataloging-in-Publication Data

Orgill, Roxane.
If I only had a horn: young Louis Armstrong / Roxane Orgill; illustrated by Leonard Jenkins.
p. cm.
Summary: Relates how the famous jazz trumpeter began
his musical career, as a poor boy in New Orleans, by singing songs on street corners
and playing a battered cornet in a marching band.
ISBN 0-395-75919-6
1. Armstrong, Louis, 1901–1971 — Juvenile literature.
2. Jazz musicians — United States — Biography — Juvenile literature.
[1. Armstrong, Louis, 1901–1971. 2. Musicians. 3. Jazz. 4. Afro-Americans — Biography.]
I. Jenkins, Leonard, ill. II. Title.
MFL3930.A75074 1997 781.65'092 — dc20 [B] 96-15380
CIP AC MN

Printed in the United States of America
HOR 10 9 8 7 6 5 4 3 2

Author's Note

There are many stories about Louis Armstrong as a boy. He told some of them himself in two published autobiographies and in countless letters and several short autobiographical writings. He was sometimes an inventive storyteller — maintaining that he was born on July 4, 1900, for example, rather than the correct but less colorful date of August 4, 1901. There are at least three stories about his first encounters with a horn. This book is based on events related in two autobiographies — *Satchmo: My Life in New Orleans* and *Swing That Music* — and in *Louis: The Louis Armstrong Story 1900–1971*, by Max Jones and John Chilton. Also consulted were Gary Giddins' *Satchmo* and James Lincoln Collier's *Louis Armstrong: An American Genius* as well as unpublished writings in the Louis Armstrong Archives at Queens College, New York. Roxane Orgill's goal was to sift through the various accounts and tell a new story that is as true as possible to the character of Louis Armstrong.

Louis opened the cupboard. Bare. He lifted the rug where his mother hid spare coins. Nothing.

"Come on," he said to his little sister, Mama Lucy. "We're going to Uncle Ike's."

At Uncle Ike's, six children were eating rice and beans out of one pot. Make that eight, with Louis and Mama Lucy. With all the clatter, Louis did not hear night slip in and wake up the city. By the time the pot was empty, music was everywhere: dancing out of door-

ways, singing on street corners, riding in from Lincoln Park on fat molecules of humid air. One sound in particular grabbed Louis by the collar. "Sounds like Joe Oliver," he said, hurrying outside.

He followed the sound to a crowd of bobbing heads
and moving feet outside the Funky Butt Hall, and yes, it
was Joe Oliver, the man they called King, crying *wah-wah*
on his cornet for all of New Orleans to hear. The snare
drum stomped out a beat that shouted "Move your feet!"

So Louis danced as if the hot blasts of music were scorching his bare feet, grinning as wide as the Big Dipper in the starry sky.

"Go, Dippermouth, go!" someone called, and Louis danced harder, because a good nickname is hard to come by, and he had just snagged a winner.

When at last the band turned and marched, not missing a beat, into the hall, he grabbed a piece of the music riding the air, to remember.

Later that night he would sit on the bed he shared with Mama Lucy and his mother, Mayann, and empty his head of all the music he had collected that day. In the dark, with his sister breathing softly beside him, he would put together a song.

If I could sing
I could bring
Home pennies
Play slow drag blues
Tap happy feet blues
Till the sun rose
If I only had a horn

Louis and his three buddies went swimming in the river where the banana boats docked. Afterward they strolled, cool and dripping, along the dock, and Big Nose Sidney started to sing. The other boys joined in, delivering a "Home Sweet Home" that was straight and true. A crowd gathered and started asking for favorite songs, and the boys sang them until their voices were no more than frog croaks and Big Nose Sidney said, "That's all folks," and passed his cap around. Louis's eyes almost popped out of his head when he saw the cap full of pennies. He filled his pockets and took off.

"Where you going, Dipper?"

"To buy rice and beans and fish heads for supper!" The boys licked their lips. Everybody knew his mother, Mayann, made the best fish-head stew in New Orleans.

"Save some for us!" But all they got was a bit of that dream song riding the breeze.

If I could sing
I could bring
Home pennies
Play slow drag blues
Tap happy feet blues
Till the sun rose
If I only had a horn

On New Year's Eve, the city of New Orleans celebrated with bang and big time. Oh, the noise! Firecrackers, hot jazz music pouring out of the honky tonks, and pistols. People shot off anything that was handy, just for the fun of it.

Louis and his gang were singing on the corner of Perdido and

Rampart Streets, collecting pennies by the capful, when a boy
fired a six-shooter from across the street.

"Go get him, Dipper!" said Big Nose Sidney. Louis pulled out an
old .38 that he had found in the bottom of his mother's trunk and
shot it six times in the air. The boy ran off like a rabbit, and Louis
and his buddies fell down laughing.

Out of nowhere a pair of strong arms grabbed Louis and shoved him into a black horsedrawn wagon with a little bitty grilled window. The wagon took Louis to jail.

There was no dream song riding the breeze that night.

Louis went to live at the Colored Waifs' Home, a place for poor boys who got into trouble. It was like no home he knew: bread and molasses for supper, and no hot jazz music filling the air, because the Home was too far from the city, and the music could not reach.

The Home had other kinds of music, though: bumblebees buzzing in the honeysuckle, boys marching with wooden guns in the courtyard, and the call of a bugle every morning and night. One day Louis discovered a roomful of boys making enough noise to blow the house down. The Waifs' Home had a band! He wanted to join on the spot, but the teacher, Mr. Davis, said he didn't need any new players, and boys from Perdido Street were nothing but trouble anyway.

Louis felt a lump inside his throat the size of a fish head, but that didn't stop him. Every day after lessons and chores he sat in a corner and listened to the band. Soon he knew all of the parts by heart.

After six long months of listening, Louis saw Mr. Davis coming toward him during supper. "Would you like to join our brass band?" he asked.

Louis was too surprised to speak.

"Wash up and come to rehearsal, then."

Running down the hall, Louis wiggled his fingers on an imaginary horn, the way he had seen Joe Oliver do.

If I could sing
I could bring
Home pennies
Play slow drag blues
Tap happy feet blues
Till the sun rose
If I only had a horn

But Mr. Davis did not give Louis a horn. He gave him a little tambourine, and then a drum. Louis rapped out a beat that made the boys tap their feet. Then he played a snappy little solo. "Hooray for Louis Armstrong!" the boys cheered.

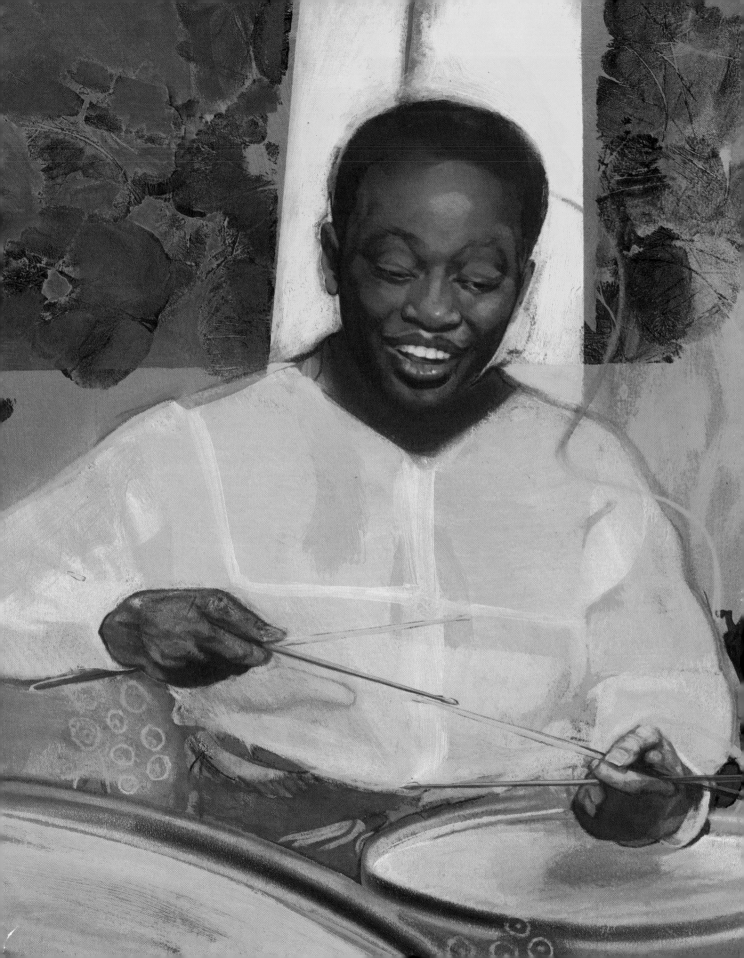

When Mr. Davis needed a new bugle boy, he chose Louis over all the others. Louis shined up the dirty old bugle so it gleamed, and at night he blew such mellow tones that the boys tumbled into bed and fell into a deep sleep.

But a bugle was not the horn Joe Oliver had used to make those *wah-wah* sounds outside the Funky Butt Hall.

"I have an awful urge to learn the cornet," Louis said to Mr. Davis.

"I know," said the teacher. "I knew the first day you burst in here. I said, 'That boy got an earful of Joe Oliver back home and he can't get rid of it. The only cure is to play the horn himself.' But you weren't ready. You thought King Oliver learned to blow like that overnight, and Bunk Johnson and Buddy Bolden, too. They didn't. They practiced." Solemnly, he took down a beat-up old cornet from a high shelf and placed the instrument in Louis's hands. "You are ready now," he said.

If I could sing
I could bring
Home pennies
Play slow drag blues
Tap happy feet blues
Till the sun rose
If I only had a horn

Louis put a battered but shiny cornet to his lips and blew. The first strains of "Home Sweet Home" shot into the air, and the Colored Waifs' Home Band marched down Perdido Street.

All the rough and tumble characters from the neighborhood appeared from nowhere and followed, dancing to the jump-happy beat.

"It's Little Louis! Find Mayann, quick!"

"Hey, Dippermouth!"

Soon everybody Louis knew had joined the second line: Uncle Ike
and his six children, Big Nose Sidney and the singing quartet, Mama
Lucy, and Mayann, waving a white handkerchief.

Mr. Davis passed a hat and it came back full to bursting with coins and dollar bills waving merrily. The band played on. The music was loud and all a jumble. Now and then Louis's cornet sent a melody spiraling up like a spinning top gone crazy. The teacher passed the hat again and again, until there was so much money that Mayann had to fetch a sack to put it all in.

Mr. Davis shouted over the noise, "Thanks to the generosity of the residents of Perdido Street, we have enough here to buy new instruments for everyone in the band." Louis took the cornet from his lips, just for a second, and grinned. Then the band turned the corner and marched down Liberty Street with Louis in the lead.